# Relieve Stress And Get Positive Thoughts

## 71 ways to reduce Cortisol



**Disclaimer**

The information provided in this book is intended for educational and informational purposes only and should not be considered as medical advice. The stress relief techniques described, including but not limited to breathing exercises, relaxation practices, and lifestyle changes, should be discussed with a qualified healthcare provider before implementation, especially if you have any pre-existing health conditions or concerns.

 Certain techniques, if not practiced correctly, may have unintended consequences, and it is essential to consult a doctor before beginning any new routine or making significant changes to your lifestyle. While these strategies may offer positive benefits, they could also have negative effects if not tailored to your individual needs. This book is not a substitute for professional medical advice, diagnosis, or treatment, and should be used in collaboration with licensed healthcare providers specializing in stress management. Always seek the advice of your doctor or other qualified health professional regarding any medical conditions or lifestyle changes.

**Introduction**

In today's world, stress has become a common companion—often showing up uninvited and lingering longer than we'd like. It doesn't discriminate, affecting people of all ages, backgrounds, and walks of life. From work deadlines and family responsibilities to financial concerns and unexpected life events, stress can pile up until it feels overwhelming. Yet, while stress is nearly unavoidable, the way we handle it can make all the difference.

The effects of stress aren't just emotional; they ripple through our physical health, mental clarity, relationships, and overall well-being. Chronic stress can lead to health issues like high blood pressure, weakened immunity, insomnia, and even depression. But more than just managing the symptoms, finding ways to reduce and handle stress effectively means embracing a balanced, thoughtful approach to living well.

## Understanding Stress

Before diving into the techniques, it's important to understand what stress is and why it can feel so intense. Stress is essentially a response to a perceived challenge or threat, activating our body's "fight or flight" system. While this response was crucial for survival in our evolutionary past, modern-day stressors often persist much longer than they were originally meant to, creating a constant sense of tension and anxiety.

Stress manifests differently for each person. For some, it may lead to physical symptoms like headaches, muscle tension, or fatigue. For others, it might cause feelings of irritability, frustration, or difficulty concentrating. By acknowledging that stress is part of the human experience, we can approach it with understanding and compassion, focusing on strategies to manage its impact rather than trying to eliminate it entirely.

## Chapter 1: Mindfulness and Relaxation Techniques

In a world full of distractions and constant demands, it's easy to get swept up in a whirlwind of stress. Mindfulness and relaxation techniques offer powerful tools to help center ourselves, clear mental clutter, and reduce daily tension. By focusing on the present moment and practicing mindful awareness, we can shift from a reactive state to a calm, intentional one. This chapter explores seven effective mindfulness and relaxation methods that can easily fit into any lifestyle, providing relief from stress and enhancing emotional well-being.

## 1. Meditation

Meditation is one of the most popular and researched techniques for achieving mental and emotional calm. By quieting the mind and focusing on a single point—whether it's the breath, a word, or a visualization—meditation helps interrupt the cycle of stress-inducing thoughts and cultivates a sense of inner peace. Regular meditation is associated with lower cortisol levels, reduced anxiety, and greater emotional resilience.

- **Mindfulness Meditation:** This technique involves focusing on the present moment, often by observing sensations or thoughts as they arise, without judgment. Practicing for even five minutes daily can help improve focus and reduce stress.
- **Guided Meditation:** Use an app or audio guide to help you through a structured relaxation or visualization process, making it easier to keep your attention on the meditation.
- **Body-Scan Meditation:** Mentally scanning your body from head to toe, releasing tension as you go, can be particularly effective for reducing physical stress and promoting relaxation.

> Tip: Set aside a few minutes each day for meditation. Consistency over time will deepen the effects of this practice.

## 2. Progressive Muscle Relaxation

Progressive muscle relaxation (PMR) is a powerful technique that involves tensing and then releasing various muscle groups to reduce physical tension. Stress often accumulates in our muscles, and PMR helps identify and release that tension, improving both physical and mental relaxation. This practice is especially helpful for unwinding at the end of the day and promoting better sleep.

- Start with your feet and work up through each muscle group, tensing each for 5-10 seconds, then releasing. Notice the sensations in your body as you relax each area.
- Focus on feeling the relaxation spread, which can reduce overall physical discomfort linked to stress.

> Try this: When you feel tension building up, take five minutes to practice PMR. You'll likely notice an immediate sense of relief and calm.

## 3. Visualization and Imagery

Visualization, or mental imagery, is a technique that uses the power of your imagination to create calm, serene images in your mind, transporting you to a peaceful place. Visualization has been shown to reduce stress and promote relaxation by diverting the mind from worry and focusing it on pleasant, calming scenarios.

  - Creating a Safe Place: Imagine a place where you feel completely relaxed—perhaps a beach, forest, or quiet room. Picture the sights, sounds, smells, and textures to fully immerse yourself in this mental space.
  - Goal Visualization: Visualize positive outcomes for specific stressors or goals. Picture yourself handling a challenging situation with confidence and ease.

> Tip: Use visualization as a quick escape during stressful moments. Just a few minutes of focused imagery can help you feel more relaxed and grounded.

## 4. Gratitude Journaling

Gratitude journaling is a powerful way to shift your mindset from stress and negativity to positivity and appreciation. Taking a few minutes to reflect on things you're grateful for can lift your mood, reduce stress, and foster an overall sense of contentment. Research shows that gratitude journaling has long-lasting effects on emotional well-being.

  - **Daily Gratitude Practice:** Each day, write down three things you're grateful for. They can be as simple as a warm cup of coffee or as significant as supportive relationships.
  - **Detailed Reflections:** Dive deeper into one of the items you're grateful for, reflecting on why it matters to you and how it enriches your life.

> Try this: Start a gratitude journal or add it to your existing journaling practice. Over time, this simple habit can build resilience and a more positive outlook.

## 5. Practicing Mindfulness in Daily Activities

Mindfulness isn't limited to meditation sessions; it can be practiced anytime by bringing awareness to your current activity. When we fully engage in our actions, we can reduce stress by quieting the "autopilot" mode that often leads to overthinking and anxiety.

   - Mindful Eating: Savor each bite, noticing the flavors, textures, and aromas of your food. Eating mindfully can improve digestion and enhance satisfaction.
   - Mindful Walking: Pay attention to the feel of your steps, the sounds around you, and the sensation of the air on your skin as you walk. Even a five-minute walk can be grounding.
   - Mindful Listening: Practice being fully present in conversations, focusing on what the other person is saying without planning your response. This not only reduces stress but also improves relationships.


## 6. Positive Affirmations

Positive affirmations are simple, uplifting statements that can shift negative thought patterns and boost self-confidence. By repeating affirmations, especially during moments of stress, you can gradually build a more positive mindset and diminish the impact of stress on your daily life.

   - Personalized Affirmations: Create affirmations that resonate with you, such as "I am capable and resilient" or "I handle challenges with ease."
   - Practice Regularly: Repeat your affirmations in the morning or before stressful situations. Writing them down in a journal can also reinforce their effects.

> Try this: Place sticky notes with affirmations in places you'll see them throughout the day, like your bathroom mirror or workspace.

## 7. Mindful Walking

Mindful walking is a moving meditation that combines the benefits of physical activity with focused awareness. Walking outdoors, especially in a natural setting, can boost mood, reduce anxiety, and provide mental clarity. Practicing mindfulness while walking allows you to fully engage your senses and momentarily disconnect from stressors.

- **Find Your Rhythm:** Walk at a comfortable pace and pay attention to the rhythm of your steps. Notice the sensations in your feet, legs, and body as you move.
- **Engage Your Senses**: Tune into your surroundings—notice the colors, sounds, and smells around you. If you're in nature, observe the movement of leaves, the sound of birds, or the warmth of the sun.
- **Release Tension:** With each step, imagine releasing stress and tension. Use your walk as a time to let go and refocus.

> Tip: Make mindful walking a regular part of your routine, especially after work or during a lunch break, to unwind and reset.

## Summary

Mindfulness and relaxation techniques offer a variety of ways to reconnect with the present moment, calm the mind, and reduce stress. Through meditation, progressive muscle relaxation, visualization, gratitude journaling, and mindful practices, you can create space in your life for peace and resilience. Start by experimenting with one or two techniques that resonate most with you. Over time, these practices can become trusted tools for managing stress and enhancing overall well-being.

## Chapter 2: Physical Activity and Exercise

Physical activity is one of the most effective ways to combat stress. Exercise not only helps release physical tension but also boosts endorphin levels, enhancing your mood and reducing cortisol, the body's primary stress hormone. Physical activities—from structured workouts to gentle stretches—can bring a sense of calm and control, helping to counteract the effects of stress on both body and mind. This chapter introduces seven physical activity techniques that are accessible to everyone and easy to incorporate into a regular routine, regardless of fitness level. You should ideally ask your doctor first if you are ready to start exercising.

## 1. Aerobic Exercise

Aerobic exercises, often referred to as "cardio," are activities that increase your heart rate and breathing for an extended period. Running, cycling, swimming, and even dancing are popular forms of aerobic exercise. Cardio activities help relieve stress by flooding the body with endorphins—also known as "feel-good" hormones—that lift mood and boost energy.

- Running or Jogging: Running can be an effective form of moving meditation. Focus on your breathing, the rhythm of your steps, or the sights around you.
- Cycling: Cycling is a low-impact activity that's gentle on the joints, making it ideal for people of all fitness levels. It's also easy to enjoy outdoors, which can further reduce stress.
- Dancing: Dancing to your favorite music is not only a great workout but also a fun way to relieve stress and lift your spirits.

## 2. Yoga for Relaxation

Yoga combines physical postures, mindfulness, and breathing exercises, making it an ideal practice for reducing stress holistically. Different forms of yoga range from gentle and restorative to more physically challenging styles, allowing you to choose an approach that suits your energy level and needs.

- Gentle or Restorative Yoga: This style focuses on slow, deliberate movements and extended stretches. It's ideal for unwinding after a long day or preparing for sleep.
- Vinyasa Flow: This form involves a sequence of poses linked with your breath, encouraging a "flow" of movement that can relieve stress and improve focus.
- Yin Yoga: Yin involves holding poses for several minutes, allowing deep relaxation

and flexibility. It's particularly effective for stress relief and quieting the mind.

## 3. Strength Training

Strength training, whether done with weights, resistance bands, or body weight, is a powerful way to combat stress. Research shows that strength training can reduce symptoms of anxiety and depression while increasing self-confidence. It also builds physical resilience, making everyday tasks feel easier and less stressful.

- **Bodyweight Exercises:** Exercises like squats, lunges, and push-ups can be done anywhere, without equipment, and are great for toning and relieving stress.
- **Free Weights:** Dumbbells or kettlebells allow you to gradually increase the weight, offering both a physical and mental challenge that's rewarding and empowering.
- **Resistance Bands:** Bands offer portable resistance training, which can be particularly useful for stretching and building strength without heavy equipment

## 4. Stretching and Flexibility Exercises

Stretching is a simple yet effective way to release muscle tension and improve flexibility, which can be particularly helpful for those who spend long hours sitting. Regular stretching not only reduces physical tension but also promotes a relaxed mind by encouraging slow, intentional movement.

- **Dynamic Stretching:** Perform these movements before exercise to warm up your muscles and increase blood flow.
- **Static Stretching:** After workouts or during breaks, hold stretches for 20-30 seconds to lengthen tight muscles and release tension.
- **Whole-Body Stretch Routine:** Focus on key areas like the shoulders, neck, and lower back—common spots for stress-related tension.

## 5. Walking in Nature

Walking is a simple, accessible exercise with profound mental health benefits. Studies show that walking, especially in natural settings, helps lower anxiety and boost mood by engaging your senses and providing a change of scenery. Walking outdoors encourages mental relaxation and allows you to connect with nature, which can help reduce stress and improve overall well-being. Consult your doctor to see if you are ready to start walking for health purposes.

  - **Forest Bathing:** Take a slow, mindful walk in a wooded area. Focus on the sights, sounds, and smells around you, allowing yourself to fully immerse in the natural environment. Being alone in the forest can be dangerous so bring a buddy and only walk on official forest hiking paths. Do not do wild hiking or walk outside areas that are known to be hiking official roads. Although relaxing it can be dangerous being alone in unknown forest area, always bring relatives or friends with you and do not walk alone in new places.
  - **Beach Walks:** Walking on sand can offer a bit of resistance, which engages the muscles while also providing a calming, rhythmic sensation. Avoid rocky areas and unknown new beaches and coastlines. Coastline hiking can be dangerous if done recklessly. Always go with a group and a hiking guide.
  - **Urban Park Strolls:** Even a walk in a city park or green space can provide a mental break and improve mood. Walk in city safe areas that are well lit in the afternoon winterly hours. Try to share this with a friend or collegue or relative and avoid walking alone.


## 6. Tai Chi and Qigong

Tai Chi and Qigong are ancient Chinese practices that involve slow, meditative movements and controlled breathing. Often described as "moving meditation," these practices help calm the mind, improve balance, and reduce physical tension. Tai Chi and Qigong are particularly helpful for people looking for a gentle, low-impact form of exercise that combines mindfulness with physical activity.

  - **Tai Chi Movements:** Tai Chi involves a sequence of slow, flowing movements that improve strength, flexibility, and balance.
  - **Qigong Exercises:** Qigong focuses on coordinating breath with gentle movement to cultivate energy and improve focus, reducing mental and physical stress.

## 7. Dancing

Dancing is a fun and expressive way to relieve stress, combining the benefits of aerobic exercise with the freedom of movement. It doesn't matter if you're an experienced dancer or a beginner; the simple act of moving your body to music can elevate mood, increase endorphins, and provide a joyful release from daily stress.

   - **Freestyle Dancing:** Put on your favorite upbeat music and dance however you feel. Freestyle dancing allows you to express emotions and connect with your body.
   - **Dance Classes:** Joining a class, whether online or in person, can be a social and structured way to get moving and learn new steps.
   - **Dance with Friends or Family:** Dance parties or even simple dances in the living room with loved ones can be a fun, shared activity that brings laughter and reduces stress.


## Summary

Physical activity is one of the most powerful tools for reducing stress, as it releases endorphins, eases muscle tension, and provides a mental break from life's demands. From cardio and strength training to gentle stretching and the simple pleasure of dancing, the options are as varied as they are effective. Start by choosing a couple of these techniques to try out, and remember that even small movements can make a big difference in how you feel. Over time, as you integrate regular physical activity into your life, you'll find yourself better equipped to handle stress with resilience, strength, and joy.


## Chapter 3: Self-Care and Personal Hobbies

Taking time for self-care and engaging in personal hobbies can be transformative in managing stress. Often, we feel overwhelmed because our time is filled with obligations, leaving little space for enjoyment and relaxation. Self-care allows us to recharge, while hobbies help bring joy, creative expression, and a sense of accomplishment. In this chapter, we'll explore eight self-care practices and hobbies that can help relieve stress and enrich your life, empowering you to approach challenges with a refreshed mind and renewed energy.

## 1. Art Therapy

Art therapy is a creative form of expression that helps process emotions, release tension, and cultivate mindfulness. You don't need to be a professional artist to enjoy the benefits—simply engaging in the creative process can lower cortisol levels, reduce anxiety, and foster a sense of accomplishment.

   - **Painting or Drawing:** Set aside time to draw or paint, focusing on the colors, shapes, and textures. Try abstract patterns, landscapes, or doodling—whatever feels natural.
   - **Coloring Books:** Adult coloring books are a great way to engage in creativity without needing special skills. The repetitive motion can be meditative and relaxing.
   - **Crafting:** Projects like pottery, jewelry-making, or scrapbooking are enjoyable ways to express creativity and provide a satisfying escape from daily stress.

> Try this: Dedicate 20-30 minutes each week to an art activity. You may find that you look forward to this time, using it as a way to unwind and express yourself freely.

## 2. Reading for Pleasure

Reading offers a mental escape, taking you out of your world and into new perspectives, places, and stories. Studies show that reading reduces stress significantly—just a few minutes spent with a good book can lower your heart rate and relieve tension. Whether you prefer fiction or nonfiction, the focus required to read helps shift your mind away from stressors.

   - **Choose Inspiring Books:** Pick up novels, self-help books, biographies, or even lighthearted magazines that bring you joy and lift your spirits.

- **Join a Book Club:** A book club adds a social component, creating a space to connect and discuss books with others.
   - **Set a Daily Reading Time:** Even reading for 10 minutes before bed can help you unwind and prepare for restful sleep.

> Tip: Keep a list of books that interest you, and set aside dedicated reading time to decompress, whether it's during a break, before bed, or over a cozy weekend.


## 3. Gardening

Gardening offers the opportunity to connect with nature, which has been shown to reduce stress, lower blood pressure, and boost mood. Tending to plants encourages mindfulness, patience, and physical movement—all of which contribute to a sense of calm and well-being.

   - Plant a Small Garden: Even a few plants on a windowsill or balcony can offer a satisfying routine of care. Herbs, flowers, or easy-to-grow vegetables can be rewarding choices.
   - Indoor Gardening: Houseplants like succulents or pothos are low-maintenance options that improve indoor air quality and bring a touch of nature indoors.
   - Get Outside: If possible, spend time in a garden, community plot, or nature space. Simply being surrounded by plants and greenery can reduce stress and lift your mood.

> Try this: Start with a small plant or two, and make tending to them a mindful activity. Observing your plants' growth and progress can be fulfilling and grounding.


## 4. Journaling

Journaling is a simple but effective way to process emotions, reflect on your thoughts, and gain clarity. It allows you to release stress by putting feelings into words, offering a healthy outlet for worries or anxieties. Regular journaling is linked to improved mental health, and it can also serve as a powerful tool for personal growth.

   - **Stream of Consciousness:** Write whatever comes to mind, without judging or

censoring. This "brain dump" technique can help clear mental clutter.
   - **Reflective Journaling:** Reflect on specific experiences, emotions, or lessons learned. Writing about positive events can improve mood and promote gratitude.
   - **Gratitude Journaling:** List three things you're grateful for each day. This practice shifts focus from stressors to sources of positivity.

> Tip: Set aside 5-10 minutes in the morning or evening for journaling. Over time, you'll develop a habit that brings clarity and a sense of calm to your day.

## 5. Cooking or Baking

Cooking and baking offer more than just nourishment—they provide a creative outlet that encourages focus, mindfulness, and enjoyment. Following recipes, measuring ingredients, and savoring the process of making a dish can be meditative and deeply satisfying. Cooking for yourself or loved ones can also foster connection, improve mood, and promote a sense of accomplishment.

 - Try New Recipes: Experimenting with different cuisines or recipes can add excitement to your routine and make mealtime something to look forward to.
 - Bake for Relaxation: Baking often requires precision, making it a great way to engage your full attention and unwind.
 - Cook with Loved Ones: Invite friends or family members to cook or bake with you for a shared, joyful experience.

> Try this: Dedicate a day each week to trying a new recipe or cooking a favorite dish with mindfulness, enjoying the textures, aromas, and tastes.

## 6. Listening to Music

Music is a powerful stress reliever that can quickly change your mood and lower anxiety. Whether you're listening to classical, pop, jazz, or any genre that resonates with you, music offers an emotional release and can improve your outlook. Engaging with music, especially music that uplifts or soothes, can be both an energizing and relaxing experience.

- **Create a Playlist:** Make playlists for different moods—one for relaxation, one for motivation, or one just for fun.
- **Discover New Music:** Exploring new genres or artists can be a fun way to take your mind off of stressors and add variety.
- **Use Music to Focus:** Instrumental or ambient music can be helpful background for tasks, promoting focus while reducing stress.

> Tip: Take a few minutes to listen to music when you feel tense. Let yourself fully immerse in the sounds and allow them to shift your mood.

## 7. Knitting or Crocheting

Knitting and crocheting are repetitive, soothing activities that can help reduce stress by focusing your mind and hands on a productive task. These crafts promote mindfulness and give you something tangible to work toward, creating a sense of accomplishment. They're ideal for quiet, meditative relaxation and can even be done in social settings.

- **Start with Simple Projects:** Beginner patterns like scarves or washcloths are a good place to start, providing a sense of satisfaction without requiring complex skills.
- **Join a Knitting Group:** Crafting with others can be a fun, social activity that also provides support and encouragement.
- **Use It as Mindful Meditation:** Focus on each stitch as a small, mindful action. Let the repetitive motion help you relax and unwind.

> Try this: Take up knitting or crocheting as a creative outlet, setting aside time in the evening to work on a project. Enjoy watching your progress as your creation takes shape.

## 8. Puzzle-Solving

Engaging in puzzles—whether jigsaw puzzles, crosswords, or Sudoku—helps shift your focus from stress to problem-solving. Puzzle-solving is a mindful, stimulating activity that encourages concentration, reducing anxiety by giving your mind a break from daily worries. It also provides a sense of accomplishment when completed, which can lift your mood.

- **Jigsaw Puzzles:** Working on a jigsaw puzzle can be an enjoyable way to spend downtime. The process of sorting pieces and forming a picture is meditative and satisfying.
- **Crosswords and Sudoku:** These classic puzzles offer mental stimulation that challenges your mind while providing a distraction from stress.
- **Puzzle Apps:** For convenience, digital puzzle apps offer a wide variety of puzzles that you can play on the go.

> Try this: Keep a small puzzle at your desk or set up a table with a jigsaw puzzle at home, returning to it when you need a quick mental break.

## Summary

Self-care and personal hobbies are valuable tools for reducing stress, allowing you to focus on activities that bring joy, peace, and a sense of accomplishment. From art and journaling to cooking and music, these practices offer time for self-expression and relaxation. Start by choosing a couple of activities that appeal to you, and make them a regular part of your life. These small but meaningful breaks will give you the energy, positivity, and mental clarity needed to face life's challenges with resilience and confidence.

## Chapter 4: Sleep and Rest (following techniques need doctor approval and any lifestyle change could have negative as well as positive outcomes, so you are safe by having a doctor approve your lifestyle change towards less stress)

Rest and quality sleep are essential for managing stress, promoting mental clarity, and maintaining physical health. When we're well-rested, we're better equipped to handle challenges, make decisions, and process emotions. Unfortunately, stress can often disrupt our sleep, leading to a cycle where lack of rest heightens stress and stress further disrupts sleep. This chapter explores five techniques to improve sleep quality, establish restful habits, and create a more relaxing sleep environment, so you can wake up feeling refreshed and ready to tackle the day.

## 1. Prioritize Sleep Hygiene

Sleep hygiene refers to habits and routines that support a healthy, consistent sleep cycle. Good sleep hygiene can significantly improve the quality and depth of your sleep, helping you feel more rested. This is especially helpful for people with busy lives who may struggle with falling asleep or staying asleep.

  - Set a Regular Sleep Schedule: Going to bed and waking up at the same time each day (even on weekends) helps regulate your body's internal clock, making it easier to fall asleep.
  - Limit Screen Time Before Bed: The blue light from screens can interfere with melatonin production, making it harder to sleep. Avoid screens for at least 30-60 minutes before bedtime.
  - Create a Relaxing Bedtime Routine: Establish relaxing rituals like reading a book, listening to calming music, or taking a warm bath to signal to your body that it's time to wind down.

> Tip: Try keeping a consistent bedtime for a week and note any changes in how you feel. Even minor improvements can make a big difference in reducing stress levels.

## 2. Power Naps for Energy and Focus

Power naps are short naps, typically lasting between 10 and 20 minutes, that can help recharge your energy and improve focus without making you feel groggy. They're especially beneficial for people who experience an afternoon energy slump or struggle to get a full night's rest. Power naps improve cognitive function and reduce stress by providing a mental and physical reset.

- Set a Timer for 10-20 Minutes: This is the ideal length for a nap, as it helps restore alertness without causing sleep inertia (the grogginess that can result from longer naps).
- Find a Quiet, Comfortable Spot: Lie down or recline comfortably in a quiet, darkened space where you won't be disturbed.
- Don't Nap Too Late in the Day: Napping after 3 p.m. can interfere with your night's sleep, so try to take naps earlier if possible.

> Try this: If you feel tired during the day, take a 10- to 20-minute nap and note any changes in your energy and focus. It can be an effective way to reduce stress and improve productivity.

## 3. Guided Sleep Meditation

Guided sleep meditations use calming instructions, soothing music, or nature sounds to help you relax and fall asleep. These meditations encourage a state of deep relaxation by guiding your mind away from anxious thoughts and into a restful state. Many people find them helpful for managing racing thoughts or winding down at the end of a stressful day.

- **Use Meditation Apps:** Apps like Calm, Insight Timer, and Headspace offer guided sleep meditations that you can listen to as you prepare for bed.
- **Listen to Nature Sounds:** Nature sounds like ocean waves, rain, or birdsong can create a serene atmosphere, blocking out distracting noises and promoting relaxation.
- **Try Progressive Muscle Relaxation:** Many guided sleep meditations include progressive muscle relaxation, where you tense and release different muscle groups to release physical tension.

> Tip: Experiment with different types of sleep meditations to find what works best for you. Some people prefer guided meditation, while others enjoy instrumental music or nature sounds.

## 4. Use of Weighted Blankets

Weighted blankets are therapeutic blankets filled with glass beads or pellets, designed to provide gentle, even pressure across the body. This pressure, known as "deep touch pressure stimulation," has been shown to reduce anxiety, lower heart rate, and improve sleep quality by promoting a feeling of calm. Many people find that using a weighted blanket helps them fall asleep faster and wake up feeling more rested.

- Choose the Right Weight: Weighted blankets are typically 5-12% of your body weight. For most people, a 10- to 15-pound blanket is ideal, but preferences may vary.
- Use It Consistently: Using a weighted blanket regularly can increase the relaxation benefits, helping you associate it with sleep and calm.
- Try It for Rest and Relaxation: You can also use your weighted blanket while relaxing, reading, or watching TV to help reduce stress and wind down in the evening.

## 5. Limit Caffeine for Better Sleep

Caffeine, while great for energy, can interfere with your sleep quality if consumed too late in the day. Even if you don't feel its effects at bedtime, caffeine can reduce the amount of deep sleep you get, which leaves you feeling less rested. Reducing or eliminating caffeine intake in the afternoon and evening can make a significant difference in your sleep quality and stress levels.

- **Switch to Decaf in the Afternoon:** Opt for decaffeinated coffee, tea, or caffeine-free herbal teas after lunchtime to ensure caffeine is out of your system by bedtime.
- **Check Hidden Sources of Caffeine:** Some sodas, chocolate, and medications contain caffeine, so be mindful of hidden sources.
- **Drink Herbal Tea in the Evening:** Calming teas like chamomile, lavender, and peppermint can promote relaxation without caffeine, helping to prepare you for sleep.

> Try this: Monitor your caffeine intake for a week, especially in the afternoon and evening, and see if cutting back improves your sleep quality.

## Summary

Getting quality rest and sleep is foundational to stress management and overall health. By establishing a consistent sleep routine, trying power naps, exploring guided sleep meditations, and considering tools like weighted blankets, you can improve your sleep quality and wake up feeling more refreshed. Start by choosing one or two of these techniques to incorporate into your life. As you get better sleep, you'll find that stress is more manageable and that you're better prepared to face the demands of each day with a clearer mind and a calmer outlook.

**Chapter 5: Diet and Nutrition**

The food and drinks we consume impact not only our physical health but also our mental well-being and ability to handle stress. Poor dietary choices, like excessive sugar, caffeine, or processed foods, can lead to mood swings, fatigue, and heightened anxiety, making it harder to cope with stress. On the other hand, certain foods and nutrients have calming effects on the mind and body, helping to stabilize blood sugar, support energy levels, and reduce tension. This chapter explores six dietary practices that can aid in stress reduction by nourishing the body and promoting balance.

**1. Limit Sugar and Processed Foods**

Sugar and processed foods may provide a quick energy boost, but they can also lead to rapid spikes and crashes in blood sugar, contributing to irritability, fatigue, and increased stress. Over time, a diet high in sugar and processed foods can also lead to chronic inflammation, which is linked to mood disorders and stress-related conditions.

   - **Choose Whole Foods**: Opt for whole, minimally processed foods like fruits, vegetables, whole grains, and lean proteins, which provide more sustained energy and stabilize blood sugar.
   - **Reduce Sugary Snacks:** Swap high-sugar snacks for healthier options like nuts, seeds, or a piece of fruit. These alternatives provide nutrients that can improve energy and mood.
   - **Read Labels:** Be mindful of hidden sugars in foods like sauces, yogurts, and cereals. Avoid ingredients like high-fructose corn syrup, which can contribute to mood swings.

> Try this: Gradually reduce your sugar intake over a week or two, paying attention to any changes in mood and energy levels. Small changes can have a significant impact on your ability to handle stress.

## 2. Stay Hydrated

Dehydration can increase feelings of fatigue and irritability, making it more challenging to manage stress effectively. Proper hydration is essential for maintaining energy levels, mental clarity, and mood stability. Even mild dehydration can contribute to symptoms of stress and anxiety, so it's essential to stay well-hydrated throughout the day. Too much water intake can be dangerous. Do not drink water too fast but sip some now and then. Research how too little water or too much water can harm you and even put you in dangerous circumstance.

  - **Drink Water Regularly:** Aim to drink at least 8 cups of water per day, or more if you're physically active. Keeping a reusable water bottle with you can help make this habit easier.
  - **Limit Caffeinated and Sugary Beverages:** Drinks like coffee, soda, and energy drinks can contribute to dehydration. Balance your caffeine intake with water.
  - **Add Flavor Naturally:** If plain water feels boring, add slices of lemon, cucumber, or berries to your water for a refreshing twist.

> Tip: Monitor your hydration levels by checking the color of your urine; it should be light yellow if you're well-hydrated. Keeping track of water intake can be a simple but powerful way to reduce stress. If your urine is like water, you are drinking too fast and too much water which is dangerous. Aim for light yellow urine.

## 3. Include Magnesium-Rich Foods

Magnesium is a mineral that plays a critical role in managing stress and relaxing muscles. Studies have shown that magnesium can help reduce anxiety and improve sleep quality, both of which are essential for stress management. Low magnesium levels are often linked with symptoms of stress, fatigue, and tension.

  - **Eat Leafy Greens:** Spinach, kale, and Swiss chard are excellent sources of magnesium. Try incorporating them into salads, smoothies, or as a side to your meals.
  - **Add Nuts and Seeds:** Almonds, cashews, sunflower seeds, and pumpkin seeds are

rich in magnesium and make for convenient, nutritious snacks.
   - **Try Avocados and Bananas:** Both are great sources of magnesium and can be easily added to meals or eaten as snacks.

> Try this: Aim to add one magnesium-rich food to each meal to keep your levels consistent throughout the day, promoting calm and relaxation.


## 4. Incorporate Adaptogenic Herbs

Adaptogens are natural herbs and roots that help the body adapt to stress and restore balance. Common adaptogens include ashwagandha, rhodiola, and holy basil, each of which can support the body's stress response. These herbs work by regulating cortisol and other stress hormones, making it easier to maintain energy levels and reduce feelings of anxiety.

   - **Ashwagandha:** Known for reducing anxiety and fatigue, ashwagandha is often taken as a supplement or added to smoothies.
   - **Rhodiola:** Rhodiola helps improve focus and mental clarity, especially during times of high stress. It can be found in supplement form or teas.
   - **Holy Basil (Tulsi):** Holy basil has calming properties and can be enjoyed as a tea for relaxation, especially in the evening.

> Tip: Always consult a healthcare provider before adding new supplements, especially adaptogens, as they may interact with certain medications or conditions.


## 5. Eat Small, Balanced Meals Throughout the Day

Large, heavy meals can lead to energy crashes, while skipping meals can cause blood sugar to drop, both of which may increase stress and irritability. Eating smaller, balanced meals throughout the day helps stabilize blood sugar, keeping energy and mood steady.

- **Focus on Balanced Macronutrients:** Aim to include a mix of protein, healthy fats, and complex carbohydrates in each meal to maintain energy levels and prevent cravings.
- **Choose Fiber-Rich Foods:** Foods high in fiber, like oats, quinoa, and sweet potatoes, slow down digestion, helping to keep blood sugar stable.
- **Snack Wisely:** Choose snacks that combine protein and fiber, like yogurt with berries or a handful of nuts, to keep hunger and energy levels in check.

> Try this: Plan your meals and snacks in advance to avoid last-minute, less healthy choices. Maintaining stable energy levels can make a big difference in managing stress.

## 6. Incorporate Probiotic-Rich Foods for Gut Health

The gut-brain connection is a well-researched link between the health of our digestive system and our mental well-being. A healthy gut microbiome can positively impact mood and stress levels, as gut bacteria produce neurotransmitters like serotonin. Probiotic-rich foods help maintain a balanced gut, which can support emotional resilience and reduce stress-related symptoms.

- **Yogurt and Kefir:** These fermented dairy products contain live cultures that support gut health. Choose options with live or active cultures for the best benefits.
- **Fermented Vegetables:** Foods like sauerkraut, kimchi, and pickles are rich in probiotics and add variety to your diet.
- **Kombucha:** This fermented tea is another probiotic-rich option, offering a refreshing way to support your gut.

> Tip: Aim to include a serving of probiotic-rich food in your diet each day. Supporting gut health is a simple, natural way to help reduce stress and improve mood.

## Summary

Nutrition plays a critical role in managing stress, with certain foods and habits offering mental and emotional benefits. By limiting sugar and processed foods, staying hydrated, incorporating magnesium-rich and adaptogenic foods, eating balanced meals, and supporting gut health with probiotics, you can build a diet that helps your body handle stress more effectively. Start by making small, mindful changes in your diet and notice the positive impact on your energy, mood, and resilience. Over time, these dietary habits can become part of a balanced, stress-free lifestyle that supports both body and mind.

## Chapter 6: Social and Emotional Support

Stress can feel isolating, but connecting with others provides comfort, perspective, and relief. Social and emotional support networks—whether friends, family, support groups, or even pets—offer reassurance and help you feel less alone in facing challenges. When we reach out to others, we tap into a source of emotional resilience that has been shown to reduce anxiety, improve mood, and even benefit physical health. This chapter explores seven ways to cultivate and benefit from social and emotional support, helping you build a strong network that can buffer you against stress.

### 1. Talk to Loved Ones

Sometimes, the simple act of sharing your thoughts and feelings with someone you trust can alleviate stress. Talking things through helps you gain perspective, feel heard, and experience a sense of relief. Social connections provide a safe space to express concerns and seek comfort without judgment.

   - **Schedule Regular Check-Ins:** Set up weekly or bi-weekly calls with a close friend or family member, creating a routine of open communication.
   - **Share Your Feelings:** Expressing what's on your mind, even if it's just for a few minutes, can help ease the emotional load.
   - **Practice Active Listening:** Engage in two-way conversations that also allow you to listen to others. Supporting each other builds stronger, reciprocal connections.

> Try this: Make it a habit to reach out when you're feeling stressed, even if it's just a quick text or phone call. You might be surprised at how much lighter you feel afterward.

## 2. Join a Support Group

Support groups, whether in person or online, provide a unique form of community where people facing similar challenges can come together. Knowing others who understand your experiences can offer comfort and validation. Support groups can be particularly helpful for those dealing with specific stressors, such as health issues, caregiving, or work-related stress.

  - **Look for Local or Online Options:** Many groups meet both in person and online, allowing you to find a setup that suits your needs and comfort level.
  - **Participate Actively:** Share your experiences, listen to others, and offer support. Contributing to the group can be just as therapeutic as receiving help.
  - **Explore Specialized Groups:** There are groups for nearly every situation—whether focused on mental health, career stress, or parenting, you'll likely find one that resonates.

> Try this: Attend a support group meeting or explore online options. Many people find relief simply by being part of a group where they feel understood and validated.

## 3. Seek Professional Therapy

A mental health professional can provide you with tools and strategies to manage stress effectively. Therapy offers a confidential, unbiased environment to explore your emotions, identify stress triggers, and develop coping mechanisms tailored to your needs. Professional therapy is particularly helpful for chronic stress, anxiety, and situations that feel too overwhelming to handle alone.

  - **Choose the Right Type of Therapy:** Different types of therapy—such as cognitive-behavioral therapy (CBT), dialectical behavior therapy (DBT), or talk therapy—address specific needs. Research which type aligns best with your goals.
  - **Find a Qualified Therapist:** Look for licensed professionals with experience in stress management or anxiety. You can ask for referrals, read reviews, or explore teletherapy options.
  - **Be Open and Honest:** Sharing your true feelings helps your therapist better understand your situation and offer tailored support.

> Tip: Therapy can be a powerful tool for building resilience, offering insights that

empower you to manage stress independently over time.


## 4. Spend Time with Pets

Animals offer unconditional companionship and emotional comfort. Studies show that spending time with pets can lower blood pressure, reduce cortisol, and release feel-good hormones like oxytocin. Petting or playing with a pet can be incredibly calming, providing a welcome distraction from daily worries and stress.

   - **Cuddle or Play with Your Pet:** Physical touch, like petting a dog or cat, can reduce tension and increase relaxation.
   - **Take Pets Outdoors:** Going for a walk with your pet, especially in nature, provides both physical activity and a mental break.
   - **Consider Animal-Assisted Therapy:** For those without pets, animal-assisted therapy programs or volunteer opportunities at shelters offer interaction with animals in a structured environment.

> Try this: Spend just 5-10 minutes each day interacting with a pet, whether playing, petting, or simply being in their presence. The companionship of a pet can lift your mood and offer immediate stress relief.


## 5. Volunteer and Help Others

Helping others can have a powerful impact on your mental health and stress levels. Volunteering fosters a sense of purpose and creates connections, reminding you that you're part of a larger community. Studies show that altruism releases endorphins and lowers stress, helping to improve mood and reduce feelings of isolation.

   - **Find Volunteer Opportunities:** Look for opportunities that align with your interests, whether it's working at a food bank, tutoring, or helping animals.
   - **Practice Kindness Daily:** Small acts of kindness, like holding the door open for someone or offering a compliment, can boost both your mood and the recipient's.
   - **Join Community Projects:** Participating in local community projects can create a sense of belonging and purpose, which is beneficial for mental well-being.

> Try this: Commit to one act of kindness or volunteering activity each week. Notice how it affects your stress levels and perspective on life's challenges.


## 6. Practice Empathy and Active Listening

Actively listening to others and practicing empathy can improve your relationships and reduce stress. By focusing on someone else's perspective, you shift your focus from your own stress and connect on a deeper level. This kind of connection can create a sense of belonging, build emotional resilience, and help you gain perspective on your own challenges.

   - **Listen Without Interrupting**: Focus fully on what the other person is saying. Practicing non-judgmental listening builds trust and strengthens connections.
   - **Validate Others' Feelings:** Acknowledge the other person's emotions, showing understanding and empathy. Saying something as simple as, "That sounds really tough," can make someone feel truly heard.
   - **Ask Open-Ended Questions:** Encourage the other person to express themselves fully, which also gives you time to reflect and connect with their experience.

> Try this: Next time you talk with a friend, focus on listening deeply and showing empathy. Strengthening connections through empathy can reduce your own stress and promote emotional resilience.


## 7. Reach Out for Help When Needed

Asking for help can be challenging, but it's a necessary part of managing stress effectively. Everyone needs support from time to time, and reaching out can lighten your load. Seeking help from friends, family, or professionals allows you to access guidance, encouragement, and practical solutions that make difficult situations more manageable.

   - **Identify Supportive People in Your Life:** Think of the people you trust who can provide reliable support, whether it's a mentor, close friend, or family member.
   - **Be Direct and Honest:** Clearly express what you need, whether it's someone to

listen, advice on a problem, or help with a task. Others are often happy to help when they know exactly what you need.

   - **Reciprocate Support:** Offer your support in return, creating a balanced relationship where both parties feel comfortable seeking help.

> Try this: The next time you feel overwhelmed, reach out to one trusted person and ask for support. Remember, seeking help is a sign of strength and can bring relief in difficult times.

**Summary**

Social and emotional support networks are vital for reducing stress and building resilience. By connecting with loved ones, joining support groups, spending time with pets, volunteering, and practicing empathy, you create a community of support that lightens your emotional load and offers comfort. Start by incorporating one or two of these practices into your life. As you strengthen your connections and lean on those around you, you'll find that stress becomes more manageable, and you'll feel more grounded in the face of life's challenges.

**Chapter 7: Organization and Time Management**

A chaotic environment or overwhelming schedule can contribute significantly to stress. Organization and time management are powerful tools for creating a sense of order, control, and peace in daily life. By breaking tasks down, setting priorities, and learning to say "no" when necessary, you can reduce stress and increase productivity. In this chapter, we'll explore seven strategies to help you organize your physical space and manage your time effectively, so you can focus on what truly matters and feel more in control of your day.

**1. Prioritize Tasks**

With so many demands on our time, it's easy to become overwhelmed. Prioritizing tasks helps you identify the most important and time-sensitive items on your to-do list, ensuring you focus on what truly needs attention. Organizing tasks by priority can reduce stress by eliminating the feeling that "everything" needs to be done at once.

- **Use the Eisenhower Matrix:** This popular time-management tool categorizes tasks into four quadrants—urgent and important, important but not urgent, urgent but not important, and neither urgent nor important. Focus on urgent and important tasks first.
- **Identify "Must-Do" vs. "Can-Do" Tasks:** Each morning, identify your top three "must-do" tasks for the day. Once these are done, move on to "can-do" items.
- **Reassess Regularly:** At the end of each day or week, review your task list. This helps you reprioritize and prevent unimportant tasks from crowding out essential ones.

> Try this: Write down your tasks for the day, then organize them based on priority. Focusing on your top tasks first can reduce stress by helping you feel accomplished and in control.

## 2. Break Down Large Tasks into Smaller Steps

Big projects or responsibilities can be overwhelming when viewed as a whole. Breaking tasks down into smaller, manageable steps can make them feel less daunting and reduce the mental barriers that cause procrastination. This approach also provides a sense of progress and accomplishment as you complete each step.

- **Create Subtasks:** Divide large tasks into actionable steps. For example, instead of "Write a report," create subtasks like "Research topic," "Outline sections," and "Write draft."
- **Set Mini-Deadlines:** Assign deadlines to each subtask to stay on track and prevent last-minute stress.
- **Celebrate Small Wins:** Acknowledge your progress after completing each step, as this can motivate you to keep moving forward.

> Tip: Use this method for any large project that feels overwhelming. You'll find that each small step brings you closer to your goal, making the process less stressful.

## 3. Use a Planner or Digital Calendar

A well-organized planner or calendar can transform the way you manage time and reduce stress associated with forgotten tasks or missed deadlines. By having a visual representation of your day, week, or month, you can better allocate time for work, personal life, and relaxation.

- **Schedule Time for Each Task:** Block out time for important tasks, meetings, and personal commitments. This prevents double-booking and ensures you have time for each responsibility.
- **Set Reminders:** Use reminders for upcoming deadlines or events. Digital planners and apps like Google Calendar allow you to set notifications to keep you on track.
- **Color-Code:** Assign different colors to various categories (e.g., work, personal, family) to quickly see how you're balancing different areas of your life.

> Try this: Spend 5-10 minutes each evening planning your next day. This simple practice can alleviate morning stress by giving you a clear sense of what to expect.

## 4. Practice Saying "No"

Setting boundaries and learning to say "no" are essential for managing time effectively. When we overcommit, we increase our stress levels and often end up unable to fully meet all obligations. Saying "no" when necessary helps protect your time and energy, allowing you to focus on the things that matter most.

- **Assess Commitments** Before Agreeing: Before saying "yes" to new responsibilities, evaluate whether you genuinely have the time and energy to take them on.
- **Use Polite Language:** Saying "no" doesn't have to feel harsh. Phrases like "I'd love to, but I'm fully booked" or "Thank you for thinking of me, but I need to pass this time" are polite yet firm.
- **Set Personal Boundaries:** Establish limits on how much time you're willing to commit to different areas of your life, and stick to them.

> Tip: Practice saying "no" to small requests initially, like minor social invitations, to build confidence in setting boundaries. As you get comfortable, it becomes easier to protect your time on a larger scale.

## 5. Set Boundaries Between Work and Personal Life

When work and personal life blur together, it's easy to feel like you're "always on," leading to burnout and heightened stress. Setting boundaries between these areas is critical for mental and emotional well-being. By clearly separating work time from personal time, you can recharge more effectively.

- **Designate Work Hours:** Establish specific work hours, even if you work from home, and try to avoid working outside of them.
- **Create a Dedicated Workspace:** Working in a set space, such as a home office, helps you mentally transition between work and personal life.
- **Limit Checking Work Messages After Hours**: Avoid checking emails or messages after work hours, as this can keep you in a work mindset and prevent you from fully relaxing.

> Try this: At the end of your workday, "close" your workspace—shut down your computer, tidy up, or move away from your desk. These small actions signal the end of work time and the beginning of personal time.

## 6. Minimize Distractions

Distractions can make tasks take longer and reduce the quality of your work, which in turn increases stress. By creating an environment that limits distractions, you can improve focus, accomplish more in less time, and enjoy a greater sense of control over your day.

- **Turn Off Notifications**: Silence notifications on your phone and computer when working on tasks that require focus. Apps like "Do Not Disturb" mode can help reduce interruptions.
- **Set Time Blocks for Focused Work**: Work in timed intervals, such as 25-minute

blocks with a short break in between, using the Pomodoro Technique. This promotes focus and helps prevent burnout.
  - **Limit Multitasking:** Multitasking can lead to errors and increased stress. Instead, focus on completing one task at a time for higher quality and faster results.

> Tip: Dedicate specific times in the day to check messages or emails rather than responding immediately. This can significantly improve your ability to concentrate.

## 7. Create a Tidy and Organized Workspace

A cluttered workspace can lead to distraction and increase stress levels. Organizing your space and keeping it clean not only saves time but also creates a calm environment where you can work or relax more effectively. An organized area promotes productivity and a sense of control.

  - **Declutter Regularly:** Set aside time to tidy up and organize your workspace. Keep only essential items within reach and store others in designated spaces.
  - **Use Organizational Tools:** Drawer organizers, shelves, and labeled folders can help keep items accessible without creating visual clutter.
  - **Personalize Your Space:** Add a few items, like photos or plants, that make the space feel inviting without overwhelming it.

> Try this: Spend five minutes at the end of each day tidying up your workspace. This small habit can make a big difference in your sense of organization and readiness for the next day.

## Summary

Organization and time management are foundational skills for reducing stress, increasing productivity, and maintaining a balanced life. By prioritizing tasks, setting boundaries, minimizing distractions, and creating an organized workspace, you can manage your day with more ease and confidence. Start by incorporating one or two of these strategies, and gradually build them into your routine. Over time, you'll find that taking control of your environment and schedule brings not only a reduction in stress but also a greater sense of fulfillment and peace.


## Chapter 8: Environmental Adjustments

Your environment has a powerful impact on your stress levels. A cluttered, noisy, or chaotic space can heighten feelings of stress and anxiety, while a clean, organized, and calming space promotes relaxation and focus. Making intentional adjustments to your environment—both at home and work—can have a significant impact on your mental well-being, providing a sense of calm and stability. In this chapter, we'll explore six strategies to create a stress-reducing environment that nurtures peace and promotes balance.


## 1. Declutter Your Space

Cluttered spaces can contribute to a cluttered mind. Studies show that physical clutter can increase stress by overwhelming our senses and making it difficult to relax. Decluttering and organizing your surroundings can create a sense of order, improve focus, and reduce mental strain.

 - **Start Small:** Tackle one area at a time, such as your desk, a kitchen counter, or a bookshelf. Breaking down the process into manageable sections prevents it from becoming overwhelming.
 - **Use the "One In, One Out" Rule**: For each new item you bring into your home or workspace, remove one that you no longer need.
 - **Regularly Purge and Organize**: Set aside time each month to reassess and remove items that no longer serve you.

> Try this: Dedicate 10 minutes each day to decluttering a small area. Gradually, this can lead to a more organized and calming environment.


## 2. Create a Calming Space

Having a designated space where you can unwind and relax can help you escape the stresses of daily life, even if it's just a small corner of your home. This "calm corner" can be a sanctuary for reading, meditating, or simply unwinding, allowing you to reset and recharge.

- **Set Up a Cozy Spot:** Use comfortable seating, soft lighting, and a few personal items, like a favorite blanket or cushion, to create a space you look forward to retreating to.
- **Add Calming Scents:** Lavender, chamomile, or sandalwood are known for their calming effects. Use candles, essential oils, or incense to infuse the space with a soothing aroma.
- **Incorporate Calming Colors**: Neutral colors like soft blues, greens, and earthy tones can create a relaxing atmosphere, helping to reduce stress.

> Tip: Designate time each day to spend in your calming space, whether it's for meditation, journaling, or simply taking a few minutes to breathe and relax.


## 3. Use Soft, Warm Lighting

Harsh, fluorescent lighting can increase stress and create a cold, sterile feeling, while softer lighting promotes relaxation and comfort. Adjusting the lighting in your environment to be warmer and more diffused can make your space feel more inviting, helping to lower stress.

- **Use Lamps with Warm Bulbs:** Rather than using overhead lights, opt for lamps with warm-colored bulbs to create a cozy atmosphere.
- **Dim the Lights in the Evening:** Dim lighting in the evening can signal to your body that it's time to unwind and prepare for sleep.
- **Try Natural Lighting:** Whenever possible, let natural light in. Exposure to natural sunlight during the day can boost mood and improve sleep quality.

> Try this: Swap out any harsh light bulbs for softer, warmer ones, especially in areas where you relax or wind down in the evening.

## 4. Turn Off Digital Notifications

Constant notifications from phones, computers, and other devices can make it feel like you're always "on," contributing to stress and making it difficult to unwind. Reducing digital distractions can provide mental space to focus, relax, and be present in your environment.

- **Silence Notifications During Downtime:** Set your phone to "Do Not Disturb" mode during meals, while working on focused tasks, or when you're relaxing.
- **Use "Focus" Settings on Your Devices:** Many devices have settings to limit notifications during specific times. Customize these to create uninterrupted time for work and relaxation.
- **Establish "No-Phone" Zones:** Designate areas in your home, like the bedroom or dining room, as device-free zones to promote connection and calm.

> Tip: Experiment with reducing notifications for just an hour each day, especially in the evening. Over time, you may find that a quieter digital environment creates a calmer mental space.

## 5. Incorporate Plants and Natural Elements

Plants not only improve air quality but also have a calming effect on the mind. Studies show that being around nature can reduce anxiety and stress, so bringing plants and other natural elements into your environment can foster a sense of peace and connection with nature.

- **Add Indoor Plants:** Low-maintenance plants like snake plants, pothos, and succulents are easy to care for and improve indoor air quality.
- **Decorate with Natural Materials:** Items made from wood, stone, or natural fibers add warmth and texture to a space, creating a calming, grounded atmosphere.
- **Create a Small Indoor Garden:** If you have the space, dedicate a small area for multiple plants, creating a mini "green corner" where you can recharge.

> Try this: Start with one or two small plants and add more over time. You'll likely notice that the simple act of caring for them can also reduce stress.


## 6. Organize Your Workspace Ergonomically

A comfortable, ergonomically designed workspace is essential for reducing physical stress and improving focus. Small adjustments to your workspace setup can prevent tension, strain, and fatigue, making it easier to stay productive and relaxed.

- **Adjust Chair and Desk Height:** Your chair and desk should be at a height that allows your feet to be flat on the floor and your arms to rest comfortably at a 90-degree angle.
- **Position Your Screen at Eye Level:** Place your computer screen at eye level to reduce neck and shoulder strain.
- **Incorporate Comfort Items:** Items like wrist rests, back supports, and footrests can make your workspace more comfortable and reduce physical stress.

> Tip: If you work from home, make small, regular adjustments to ensure your workspace is comfortable. Your body will thank you, and you'll feel less stressed by the end of the day.


## Summary

The environment you surround yourself with plays a critical role in managing stress and creating a sense of calm. By decluttering, setting up a calming space, adjusting lighting, limiting digital distractions, bringing in natural elements, and optimizing your workspace ergonomically, you can create a sanctuary that supports mental clarity and relaxation. Start by making one or two small changes, and as you experience the benefits, continue to adapt your environment to best support your well-being. A peaceful environment fosters a peaceful mind, giving you the mental space to handle life's challenges with more balance and ease.

## Chapter 10: Alternative and Holistic Practices

Holistic and alternative practices can offer unique approaches to stress relief by addressing the mind, body, and spirit as interconnected. Many of these practices have been used for centuries in cultures around the world to promote balance and well-being, and they are increasingly supported by modern research for their ability to reduce stress, improve focus, and enhance relaxation. In this chapter, we'll explore seven alternative practices that can complement traditional stress management techniques, providing additional ways to find calm and center yourself.

### 1. Acupuncture

Acupuncture is an ancient Chinese therapy that involves inserting fine needles into specific points on the body to stimulate energy flow and restore balance. Acupuncture can reduce stress by promoting the release of endorphins and lowering cortisol levels, helping to relieve physical and mental tension. It's often used for pain relief, but it's also effective in calming the mind and promoting a sense of relaxation.

- **Find a Licensed Practitioner:** It's important to seek treatment from a qualified, licensed acupuncturist to ensure a safe and effective experience.
- **Consider Consistent Sessions:** Regular acupuncture sessions are often recommended to experience sustained benefits for stress relief.
- **Combine with Deep Breathing:** While receiving treatment, practice deep breathing to enhance the relaxation response and maximize the session's benefits.

> Tip: If you're curious about acupuncture, start with one session to see how it affects you. Many people find it surprisingly relaxing, even after the first visit.

## 2. Massage Therapy

Massage therapy helps relieve physical tension and relaxes the nervous system, making it a popular choice for stress relief. Through touch, massage stimulates the release of dopamine and serotonin—both of which are known to improve mood and reduce anxiety. Regular massage therapy can also alleviate muscle pain caused by stress, leaving you feeling both mentally and physically relaxed.

- **Choose the Right Type of Massage:** Swedish, deep tissue, and Thai massage are popular options. Swedish massage is gentle and relaxing, while deep tissue massage targets specific areas of tension.
- **Incorporate Aromatherapy Oils:** Adding calming essential oils like lavender or eucalyptus can enhance relaxation during the massage.
- **Practice Self-Massage:** Simple techniques like massaging your neck, shoulders, or hands can provide relief between professional sessions.

> Try this: Schedule a massage once a month or incorporate self-massage techniques into your routine. Physical touch can be incredibly grounding and stress-relieving.

## 3. Aromatherapy

Aromatherapy uses essential oils derived from plants to promote relaxation, reduce anxiety, and improve mood. When inhaled, essential oils stimulate the olfactory system, which influences the brain's limbic system and can trigger a calming response. Different oils are known for specific effects, and they can be used in various ways to suit your preferences.

- **Try Lavender for Calming:** Lavender oil is widely known for its soothing effects and can help promote relaxation and better sleep.
- **Use a Diffuser:** Essential oil diffusers allow you to gently scent a room, creating a calming environment. You can use blends like chamomile, cedarwood, and ylang-ylang to ease stress.
- **Apply Topically:** Dilute a few drops of essential oil with a carrier oil (like coconut or almond oil) and apply to your wrists, temples, or neck for portable stress relief.

> Tip: Experiment with different essential oils to find ones that resonate with you. Scents like eucalyptus, bergamot, and frankincense are also popular for their relaxing properties.


## 4. Float Therapy

Float therapy, or sensory deprivation, involves lying in a dark tank filled with water and Epsom salt that allows you to float effortlessly. This creates a weightless environment that removes external stimuli, allowing your mind and body to deeply relax. Float therapy is known for its ability to reduce stress, ease muscle tension, and promote mindfulness by giving you an opportunity to fully disconnect.

   - **Prepare for the Experience:** Many people find their first float unfamiliar, but deep relaxation comes easier with practice. Relax your body and focus on your breathing.
   - **Let Go of Expectations:** Simply focus on being present, without trying to achieve anything specific. The absence of sensory input allows your mind to reach a state of calm naturally.
   - **Focus on Breath Awareness:** In the quiet space, breathing slowly and deeply can deepen your relaxation and keep you grounded in the present.

> Try this: Book a float session when you feel particularly stressed or anxious. Many people find it to be a unique experience that provides deep relaxation and mental clarity.


## 5. Breathwork Techniques

Breathwork involves intentional breathing patterns to promote mental, emotional, and physical well-being. By focusing on different rhythms and intensities of breath, breathwork exercises can lower stress, increase oxygen flow, and shift you out of a "fight or flight" response. This practice is often used in both modern and ancient wellness traditions to calm the nervous system and clear the mind.

   - **Try Box Breathing:** Inhale for a count of four, hold for four, exhale for four, and pause for four. This balanced breathing pattern is calming and can be used anytime.

- **Practice Alternate Nostril Breathing:** This technique, often used in yoga, involves closing one nostril while breathing in and then switching nostrils for the exhale. It helps balance the mind and calm stress.
- **Explore Holotropic Breathwork:** This more advanced technique uses faster breathing patterns to reach a meditative state and release pent-up emotions.

> Tip: Incorporate a simple breathwork technique into your daily routine. Even just five minutes of focused breathing can significantly reduce stress levels.

## 6. Reiki and Energy Healing

Reiki is a form of energy healing that originated in Japan. It involves a practitioner placing their hands just above or lightly on the body, with the intention of channeling healing energy to balance and clear energy blocks. Reiki and other energy healing practices promote relaxation, relieve physical tension, and help balance the mind and emotions.

- **Find a Certified Practitioner:** Reiki is most effective when performed by a trained practitioner who understands energy healing techniques.
- **Be Open to the Experience:** Reiki is a gentle, non-invasive practice. Approach it with an open mind, and allow yourself to simply receive.
- **Try Self-Reiki:** Learning basic self-Reiki techniques can allow you to practice energy healing on yourself, focusing on areas where you feel tension or stress.

> Tip: Schedule a Reiki session when you feel emotionally drained or physically tense. Many people report feeling deeply relaxed and lighter after sessions.

## 7. Exploring CBD and Herbal Supplements

CBD (cannabidiol), derived from the hemp plant, and other herbal supplements can help relieve stress, promote relaxation, and improve sleep. CBD is non-psychoactive and works by interacting with the body's endocannabinoid system to regulate stress response, while other herbs like valerian root and chamomile are also known for their calming effects. It's important to research dosage and consult a healthcare provider before starting new supplements. **<u>ALWAYS USE SUPPLEMENTS UNDER THE ADVICE OF A</u>**

<u>**DOCTOR**</u>

   - **Try CBD Oil or Capsules:** Start with a low dose to see how your body responds, and consider using it in the evening to promote relaxation and restful sleep.
   - **Explore Herbal Teas:** Chamomile, valerian root, and lemon balm teas can help reduce stress and calm the mind without the need for supplements.
   - **Consider Adaptogens:** Adaptogenic herbs like ashwagandha and rhodiola help the body adapt to stress over time, building resilience.

> Tip: Incorporate herbal supplements into your routine gradually, and monitor how they affect your stress levels and overall sense of calm.


## Summary

Alternative and holistic practices offer a diverse range of tools for managing stress and achieving a deeper sense of calm and balance. Whether through the physical relief of acupuncture and massage, the sensory escape of float therapy, or the energy harmonization of Reiki, these practices invite you to explore new ways of restoring peace to both mind and body. Start by trying one or two techniques that resonate with you and, over time, build a toolkit of practices that work in harmony with your life. These holistic approaches can complement traditional stress management techniques, providing you with a well-rounded approach to managing stress with intention and care.


## Chapter 11: Positive Lifestyle Habits

Incorporating positive lifestyle habits into your daily routine can improve your resilience to stress, enhance your mood, and support overall well-being. Simple yet powerful habits, such as acts of kindness, lifelong learning, and making time for fun, can help shift your focus from stressors to sources of fulfillment and joy. These habits create a foundation of positivity that strengthens your ability to handle life's challenges with greater ease and optimism. In this chapter, we'll explore six positive lifestyle habits that can naturally reduce stress and lead to a more fulfilling life.

## 1. Practice Kindness and Small Acts of Generosity

Acts of kindness, whether big or small, can reduce stress and boost happiness by shifting your focus outward. Helping others releases endorphins and oxytocin, hormones that promote positive feelings and reduce cortisol. When we engage in generosity, we create positive interactions that not only improve our own well-being but also strengthen our connections with others.

- **Practice Random Acts of Kindness:** Hold the door open, pay for someone's coffee, or leave a kind note for a coworker. These small gestures can brighten someone else's day and lift your own mood.
- **Volunteer Your Time:** Volunteering offers a way to contribute to a cause you care about while connecting with others. It's a structured way to bring purpose and positivity into your life.
- **Practice Daily Kindness:** Make kindness a habit by committing to one small act of kindness each day. This could be as simple as complimenting someone or sending a thoughtful message.

> Try this: Keep a kindness journal where you record acts of kindness you give and receive. Reflecting on these moments can reinforce positivity and make kindness a regular part of your life.

## 2. Engage in Lifelong Learning

Learning something new provides mental stimulation, which can reduce stress by engaging the mind in positive, goal-oriented activities. Lifelong learning encourages a growth mindset, helping you view challenges as opportunities for development rather than as stressors. Exploring new interests also builds confidence and brings a sense of accomplishment.

- **Take Up a New Hobby**: Whether it's photography, cooking, or gardening, learning a new hobby can boost your creativity and provide a refreshing break from daily routines.
- **Join a Class or Workshop:** Look for local or online classes in topics that interest you. From painting to coding, the options are limitless and can be tailored to fit your schedule.
- **Read Books on New Subjects:** Reading expands your knowledge and keeps your mind active. Try exploring genres or topics outside your usual interests.

> Try this: Set a goal to learn one new thing each month, whether it's through a book, a video tutorial, or a workshop. Lifelong learning keeps you curious and engaged, reducing the monotony that can sometimes contribute to stress.

## 3. Schedule Time for Fun and Play

Many people underestimate the power of fun and playfulness in reducing stress. Making time for enjoyment helps you reconnect with your inner child, lightening your mood and releasing endorphins. Fun activities provide mental and emotional breaks from responsibilities, allowing you to relax and recharge.

- Plan Fun Outings or Activities: Schedule time for activities you enjoy, such as hiking, attending a concert, or going to a museum. Regularly planned "fun time" can be as important as other obligations.
- Laugh Often: Laughter has been shown to reduce cortisol and release endorphins. Watch a comedy, spend time with funny friends, or try laughter yoga to lift your spirits.
- Incorporate Playfulness into Daily Life: Approach simple activities with a playful attitude. Even something as routine as cooking can become more enjoyable if you play music and try out new recipes.

> Tip: Treat fun activities like any other appointment by blocking off time in your calendar. Scheduling fun ensures that you prioritize it and make it a regular part of your life.

## 4. Focus on Your Accomplishments

Recognizing your achievements, even small ones, can build confidence and reduce stress by reinforcing a positive mindset. When we focus on what we've accomplished rather than what remains undone, we shift to a more optimistic outlook, which can help us tackle challenges with resilience and positivity.

- **Keep an Accomplishment Journal:** Each day, write down one or two things you achieved. These can be small wins, like completing a task or sticking to a new habit.
- **Reflect on Your Progress Regularly:** Set aside time weekly or monthly to review your accomplishments. This reflection helps you recognize your growth and stay

motivated.
- **Celebrate Milestones:** Marking milestones, even minor ones, reinforces a sense of progress. Treat yourself to something special, like a nice meal or a fun outing, to celebrate.

> Try this: Create a list of your achievements over the past year. Recognizing the progress you've made can provide encouragement and help you appreciate your efforts, reducing the stress of constantly feeling like you "need to do more."

## 5. Limit Screen Time

Excessive screen time, especially on social media or news sites, can increase stress by exposing you to a constant stream of information and comparison. Limiting screen time allows you to be more present, connect with the people around you, and reduce mental clutter. Reducing screen exposure, particularly before bed, can also improve sleep quality.

- **Set Daily Screen Time Limits:** Use apps or built-in device features to track and limit your screen time, especially on social media or non-essential apps.
- **Establish a "Tech-Free" Zone:** Designate areas in your home, like the dining room or bedroom, as tech-free zones to encourage offline interaction and relaxation.
- **Take Regular Breaks from Screens:** Follow the 20-20-20 rule: Every 20 minutes, look at something 20 feet away for at least 20 seconds. This reduces eye strain and mental fatigue.

> Try this: Spend the first hour of your day and the last hour before bed without screens. Instead, focus on activities like reading, journaling, or stretching to promote a more relaxed and mindful start and end to your day.

## 6. Celebrate Small Victories and Moments of Joy

Focusing on the positive moments and small victories in your life can significantly improve your outlook and reduce stress. When we stop to recognize even the smallest wins, we cultivate a sense of gratitude and mindfulness that makes everyday life feel more fulfilling.

Celebrating small victories reinforces a positive mindset, helping us stay motivated and resilient.

- **Notice Daily Moments of Joy:** Throughout the day, take mental note of moments that bring you happiness, whether it's a good cup of coffee, a kind gesture, or a personal achievement.
- **Create a "Joy Jar":** Write down small victories and positive moments on slips of paper and collect them in a jar. When you're feeling stressed, read a few to remind yourself of life's good moments.
- Acknowledge Your Progress Regularly: Reflect on your progress and celebrate it, even if it's small. Recognizing growth, no matter how gradual, keeps you motivated and reduces stress.

> Tip: Set aside a few minutes each day to reflect on your wins. Celebrating small victories reminds you that each day has positive moments, making stressors feel more manageable.

## Summary

Incorporating positive lifestyle habits into your routine builds a foundation of resilience, joy, and well-being that supports you through life's challenges. By practicing kindness, engaging in lifelong learning, scheduling time for fun, acknowledging accomplishments, limiting screen time, and celebrating small victories, you create a life filled with meaning, connection, and balance. Begin by integrating one or two of these habits, and gradually build a routine that reflects your values and passions. Embracing these habits will help you approach life with optimism and gratitude, reducing stress and enriching your everyday experience.

## Chapter 12: Therapeutic and Professional Help

There are times when managing stress on your own becomes challenging, and seeking professional support can be a transformative step toward relief and healing. Therapeutic and professional help offers tailored strategies, expert guidance, and structured tools for handling stress, building resilience, and addressing underlying issues. Mental health professionals, including therapists, counselors, and medical practitioners, are trained to provide the support and insights needed to navigate complex stressors. This chapter explores five types of therapeutic and professional support that can help you manage stress effectively and sustainably.

## 1. Cognitive-Behavioral Therapy (CBT)

Cognitive-Behavioral Therapy (CBT) is a widely used, evidence-based approach to treating stress, anxiety, and depression. CBT focuses on identifying and challenging unhelpful thought patterns and replacing them with constructive ways of thinking. This therapy is particularly effective for stress management, as it provides tools for reframing negative thoughts, managing emotions, and responding to stressors more calmly.

- **Identify Negative Thought Patterns:** In CBT, a therapist helps you recognize patterns of thinking, such as catastrophizing or all-or-nothing thinking, that contribute to stress.
- **Learn Practical Coping Skills:** CBT includes strategies like thought-stopping, positive self-talk, and mindfulness techniques that you can use in stressful situations.
- **Set and Achieve Goals:** CBT often involves setting specific, manageable goals for behavioral change, which can help build confidence and reduce stress over time.

> Tip: Look for a licensed CBT therapist, as CBT is most effective when practiced under the guidance of a trained professional.

## 2. Biofeedback Therapy

Biofeedback therapy is a technique that uses real-time monitoring of physiological functions—such as heart rate, muscle tension, and breathing patterns—to teach individuals how to control these responses. Biofeedback can help reduce stress by giving you insight into how your body responds to stress and teaching you how to manage these responses consciously.

- **Monitor Physical Responses:** During a session, sensors are attached to your body to measure physiological signals, which are displayed on a monitor for you to observe.

- **Learn to Control Stress Responses:** With the help of a biofeedback therapist, you learn techniques to control your heart rate, breathing, or muscle tension in response to stress.
  - **Practice Self-Regulation**: Over time, you can apply the relaxation techniques learned in biofeedback to everyday stressful situations, leading to greater control over stress responses.

> Try this: Look for biofeedback centers or clinics that specialize in stress management to explore this method. Many people find biofeedback to be empowering and effective for reducing stress.


## 3. Dialectical Behavior Therapy (DBT)

Originally developed for borderline personality disorder, Dialectical Behavior Therapy (DBT) has proven effective for managing intense emotions, stress, and interpersonal challenges. DBT combines acceptance strategies with behavioral techniques, making it particularly helpful for those who experience high levels of stress and find it difficult to regulate emotions.

  - **Learn Mindfulness Skills:** DBT emphasizes mindfulness as a way to stay present and reduce stress by observing thoughts and feelings without judgment.
  - **Develop Emotion Regulation Skills:** DBT includes practical tools to help manage intense emotions and decrease stress by understanding emotional triggers.
  - **Build Interpersonal Effectiveness:** DBT teaches communication strategies that reduce conflict and enhance relationships, creating more positive interactions that lower stress.

> Tip: If you experience chronic stress or emotional dysregulation, DBT can be very beneficial. Look for a certified DBT therapist or a DBT group program.


## 4. Eye Movement Desensitization and Reprocessing (EMDR)

EMDR is a therapeutic approach used primarily for trauma and post-traumatic stress, but it has also been shown to reduce stress and anxiety related to difficult past experiences.

Through structured eye movements or other bilateral stimulation, EMDR helps process and reframe distressing memories, reducing their emotional intensity and impact on current stress levels.

- **Process Past Experiences:** EMDR helps you revisit and process unresolved experiences that may still trigger stress responses.
- **Reframe Negative Beliefs**: During EMDR, you work with a therapist to replace negative beliefs associated with the memories with more empowering, positive ones.
- **Reduce Emotional Sensitivity:** After several sessions, many people report that previously distressing memories no longer trigger intense stress reactions.

> Try this: Consider EMDR if you feel that past experiences or trauma are contributing to your stress. A trained EMDR therapist can guide you through the process safely.

## 5. Medication and Medical Support

For some people, stress can reach levels where medication is beneficial, particularly if it contributes to anxiety, depression, or sleep issues. Medications prescribed by a qualified healthcare provider can help manage symptoms, making it easier to benefit from other stress management practices. While medication is not a standalone solution, it can be an effective tool in a comprehensive stress management plan.

- **Consult a Psychiatrist or Physician:** Only qualified medical professionals should prescribe medication for stress, anxiety, or related conditions.
- **Consider Short-Term Support:** Some medications are intended for short-term use to manage acute symptoms, allowing you time to establish coping strategies.
- **Combine with Therapy:** Medications are most effective when paired with therapy or other stress management techniques, as these address the root causes of stress.

> Tip: If you're considering medication, have an open conversation with a healthcare provider to discuss potential benefits, risks, and alternatives. They can help you develop a balanced plan that supports your mental health and overall well-being.

**Summary**

Therapeutic and professional help provides valuable tools and support for managing stress, particularly when stress feels overwhelming or persistent. Cognitive-behavioral therapy, biofeedback, dialectical behavior therapy, EMDR, and medication each offer unique benefits, addressing stress from different angles and supporting emotional resilience. Seeking help from a professional is a proactive step toward understanding and managing your stress in a sustainable way. Integrate these options with your other self-care and stress-reducing practices, and remember that asking for help is a powerful and positive choice on your journey to a balanced, healthy life.

## Chapter 13: Creative Expression

Creative expression allows you to release stress, tap into your inner world, and explore emotions in a safe, unstructured way. Artistic activities like painting, writing, singing, or dancing offer a powerful outlet for processing feelings, which can help reduce anxiety and improve mood. You don't need to be a professional artist to benefit from creativity; the act of creating itself is therapeutic. In this chapter, we'll explore six forms of creative expression that can help you reduce stress and discover a new side of yourself.

### 1. Creative Writing and Journaling

Writing provides a structured way to process emotions, gain perspective, and clear your mind. Creative writing, such as storytelling or poetry, allows for self-expression, while journaling is a powerful tool for reflecting on thoughts, emotions, and personal growth. Both forms of writing can reduce stress by helping you articulate feelings and make sense of your inner world.

   - **Stream-of-Consciousness Writing:** Set a timer for 5-10 minutes and write whatever comes to mind without censoring yourself. This "brain dump" can be liberating and provide insight.
   - **Daily Journaling Practice:** Reflect on your day, emotions, and any stressors you experienced. Writing helps you process events and release worries onto paper.
   - **Explore Storytelling:** Write a short story or poem that reflects an emotion or situation you're experiencing. This can provide emotional distance and offer new perspectives.

> Tip: Keep a journal by your bedside or in your bag for easy access. Regularly writing, even for a few minutes, can reduce stress and enhance self-awareness over time.

## 2. Drawing, Painting, and Visual Art

Visual art is an intuitive way to release emotions and engage in the creative process without the need for words. Drawing, painting, and other forms of visual art allow you to express feelings non-verbally, helping you focus on the present moment and reduce stress. Art therapy is even used clinically to help people process emotions and gain mental clarity.

- **Start with Simple Sketching:** Grab a sketchbook and pencil and start with simple shapes, doodles, or patterns. The repetitive motion can be meditative and relaxing.
- **Experiment with Colors and Textures:** Colors can evoke different emotions, so explore with vibrant or soothing colors based on your mood. Try different materials, like watercolors or pastels.
- **Create Abstract Art:** Don't worry about "making it perfect." Abstract art allows for free expression without boundaries, making it ideal for stress relief.

> Try this: Set aside 15-20 minutes to create something without any specific goal. Allowing yourself to explore freely can bring relaxation and joy to the creative process.

## 3. Music and Singing

Music is deeply connected to emotion and can have an immediate impact on mood. Listening to music that resonates with you, playing an instrument, or singing can help you release stress, shift your emotional state, and connect with yourself on a deeper level. Music therapy is widely used for stress relief, as it helps reduce anxiety and create positive, calming experiences.

- **Create Playlists for Different Moods:** Make playlists that help you relax, feel energized, or lift your spirits. Having a go-to playlist for stressful moments can be incredibly comforting.

- **Learn a Musical Instrument:** Playing an instrument requires focus, which can take your mind off stress and immerse you in the present moment. Even beginners can benefit from this creative outlet.
- **Sing Freely:** Singing, whether in the shower or along with your favorite songs, releases endorphins and can quickly elevate mood. It's an expressive way to feel a sense of release.

> Tip: Try singing or playing music as a daily practice, even for just a few minutes. You may find it instantly improves your mood and relieves tension.


## 4. Dance and Movement

Dance allows you to connect with your body, express emotions physically, and enjoy a sense of freedom. Movement has been shown to lower cortisol levels and release endorphins, and the act of dancing can feel joyful and liberating. Dance doesn't have to be structured; even free-form movement can provide an emotional and physical release from stress.

- **Try Free-Form Dance:** Put on music you love and let your body move however it wants. Focus on the rhythm and how your body feels, letting go of any judgments.
- **Follow Online Dance Classes:** If you prefer structure, many online dance classes cater to beginners and allow you to try different styles from the comfort of home.
- **Incorporate Dance Breaks:** Take a quick dance break during your day whenever you feel stressed or tired. Even a short dance session can reenergize you and clear your mind.

> Try this: Set aside 5-10 minutes each day to dance freely. Use this time to let go of stress and connect with your body in a playful way.


## 5. Photography and Nature Exploration

Photography combines the art of observation with the calming effects of nature. Taking photos of the world around you encourages mindfulness and helps you appreciate beauty in the details. Nature photography, in particular, reduces stress by connecting you with the outdoors and encouraging you to focus on what's around you rather than on your worries.

- **Practice Mindful Photography:** Walk around and capture photos of details you find interesting or beautiful. Focus on textures, colors, or the way light falls.
- **Explore Nature Photography:** Head outdoors and capture natural landscapes, plants, or wildlife. This combines the calming effects of nature with creative focus.
- **Create a Visual Diary:** Document your daily life or special moments through photos. A visual diary allows you to look back on positive moments, helping reinforce a sense of gratitude.

> Tip: Use your phone or a camera to capture one or two photos each day. Reflecting on these images can remind you of the beauty and calm present in everyday life.


## 6. Theater and Role-Playing

Theater and role-playing can be powerful outlets for exploring emotions, building confidence, and letting go of stress. Acting allows you to express different sides of yourself, process experiences, and see life from new perspectives. Even if you're not interested in formal theater, casual role-playing or acting exercises can offer similar stress-relieving benefits.

- **Try Improv Exercises:** Improvisational exercises are fun and spontaneous, encouraging you to think quickly and express yourself freely without judgment.
- **Reenact Stressful Situations with a Positive Twist:** Role-play stressful scenarios in a new light, perhaps acting them out as though they went well. This can help you reframe difficult experiences.
- **Attend or Join a Theater Group**: If you enjoy performing, consider joining a local theater group. Acting in a supportive group setting can help you build community and reduce stress.

> Tip: Role-playing with friends or acting out scenes from your imagination can be a fun, playful way to process emotions and reduce stress. Let yourself experiment without taking it too seriously.

Summary

Creative expression is a powerful tool for managing stress, allowing you to connect with your inner self, explore emotions, and shift your focus from stressors to sources of joy and fulfillment. From writing and visual art to music, dance, photography, and theater, these forms of creativity offer a variety of outlets for relaxation and self-discovery. Start by choosing one or two forms of creative expression that resonate with you, and dedicate regular time to explore them. As you engage in these creative practices, you'll likely find that they become a meaningful and joyful part of your stress-relief toolkit. Through creativity, you can experience both freedom and healing, transforming stress into inspiration and self-growth.

## Conclusion

Congratulations on taking this journey through 81 Ways to Reduce Stress! By exploring these diverse strategies, you've equipped yourself with powerful tools to navigate life's challenges with resilience, calm, and a renewed sense of joy. Remember, stress is a natural part of life—but with the right techniques, you can transform it into a source of growth, inspiration, and strength. Each chapter of this book offers something unique, whether it's cultivating mindfulness, engaging in creative expression, finding balance through organization, or tapping into the power of social connections. These practices are here to support you every step of the way.

Think of your stress-management journey as an evolving toolkit, filled with techniques you can mix and match to suit your needs. Some days, you might find comfort in meditation or a simple walk in nature; on other days, creativity or a supportive conversation with a friend could be just what you need. There's no one-size-fits-all solution, and that's what makes this journey exciting. The more you try, the more you learn about what works best for you.